ELITE RACING CLUB

the book

Elite Racing Club
P.O.Box 100, Devizes, Wiltshire, SN10 4TE

ISBN 1873313063

Acknowledgements
Dan Downie, Claire Benson, Sue Hart, Matthew Budden,
Oscar Yeadon, David Clark, James Pithie, Martin Hill, Tim Hanlon

Published by Elite Racing Club, P.O. Box 100, Devizes, Wiltshire, SN10 4TE

CONTENTS

Lumberjack (bottom right)

Elite Racing Club began in December 1992. It was financed by Elite Registrations, who, at the time, were Britain's leader in the trading of personalised car registrations. The Department of Transport had thrown a gigantic spanner in the works by joining the marketplace and instantly assuming the number one position. It made so much sense to diversify.

The company already owned a racehorse, named Elite Reg, trained by Paul Cole, at Whatcombe (near Lambourn). The colt was not exactly star material on the Flat, so he was switched to a National Hunt career with new and ambitious trainer Charles Egerton. After his Flat career came to an end, Charles managed to get the horse jumping and entered him at Exeter. The trouble was that it was a Claiming Race and after 'Reggie' ran the race of his life, just beaten on the line, he was claimed by Martin Pipe and the rest was history, as Reggie went on to win race after race for the champion trainer and his new owner.

Losing "Reggie" was the spark that ignited the fire and Elite Racing Club was launched there and then.

The first horse to be purchased was an attractive chaser called Lumberjack and he went to Charles Egerton's yard. It was almost a fairy tale start for the Club, when at Newton Abbot in January 1993, Lumberjack, under Richard Dunwoody, looked the likely winner turning out of the back straight, but he was overhauled close home and finished a creditable second.

The next purchase was the beautifully bred filly Kabayil (by Dancing Brave). She was a winner on the Flat and was sent to the sales by her wealthy Arab owner. The bidding was fast and furious and we went that 'extra mile' to secure her for £16,000. She also went to Charles Egerton's yard.

In February 1993, Kabayil went to Plumpton racecourse and was first past the post on her debut. She became the Club's first ever winner. It was a thrilling moment for everyone connected.

Kabayil

Originally, the Club colours were; white jacket with pink star and yellow cap but these were quickly changed to the well known white jacket with three large black spots and a black cap.

Little did we realise back in 1992 that Elite Racing Club would become Britain's leader or that our first ever winner (Kabayil) would become a leading light in our breeding programme, ten years later.

Neither did we know that our success would lead to a vast number of 'copycat' racing clubs. In fact, there was a point when one new Club was starting every week. The majority of these have now fallen by the way-side, because perhaps, they perceived the business to be a glamorous money making venture. The truth is that the expenses are huge and it requires a large amount of manpower to run. However, we did have a trading advantage in the early days, when we utilised the administrative facilities, and financial support of Elite Registrations. We would like to think that, generally, both the racing club business and racehorse syndicate business have benefited from our success.

Our target is to maintain an average figure of twenty horses in training. The average throughout 2002 was more like 23.

Having a large quantity, is (almost) a guarantee that there will be all-year action. More importantly, the greater the number of horses that pass through, the greater chance there is of finding a star performer.

Ten years ago we told prospective new members that the dream was for the Club to own a Group 1 winner. It probably sounded far fetched at the time, but it was always a serious target. On 28th September 2002, that dream became reality with Soviet Song. Elite Racing Club had joined the premier division!

Dancing Bay

Very few people of sound mind would ever sell a mare that they knew would definitely produce a Group 1 winner. Given that most owners of racehorses are wealthy, it is rare that they would sell for financial reasons. Of course, in the real world, there's no guarantee that a mare will successfully produce any offspring, let alone a winner and most emphatically, let alone a Group 1 winner.

The majority of racehorses that are sold as broodmares are not likely to produce above average offspring. Maybe about 10% will do so, but less than 0.1% will produce a Group 1 winner. Keep in mind, that the majority of the best prospects are not sent to the sales, but when a star name does go under the hammer, the wealthy Arabs will be swarming around the honey pot and they will not be flinching when the bidding hits a million. Mind you, when they sniff the prospect of acquiring a star, quite often, a private deal will bypass the sale ring altogether.

Whilst there's no exact science to producing quality offspring, beyond doubt, you can improve your chances considerably if you match a quality sire with a quality mare.

We would of course, like to acquire a leading sire, but for the moment that is yet another dream.

This knowledge will help you understand why we have been carefully selecting which mares to retain and introduce to our breeding programme, once retired from racing.

Selecting a sire to pair with, is the most contentious issue of the process. Our breeding programme is a team effort and views will vary. Primarily, the task is to choose a sire with a winning record over a similar distance to that of the mare. Then there's the question of the likelihood of producing an early sort etc..... Are we breeding for Flat or National Hunt? The list goes on. Not forgetting, of course, that the cost of a nomination is an important factor. There isn't a bottomless pit of money.

Boston Lodge

The Club's breeding programme began with the purchase of a brood-mare called Corman Style (Ahonoora), back in 1994. She was already in foal (to Primo Dominie) and produced our first homebred, a colt named Domino Style. Her third foal, Most Stylish, was a dual winner for the Club.

Dixie Favor (Dixieland Band) became our second broodmare. On paper, she looked better than Corman Style and indeed, her first foal was a winner (Stately Favour).

It wasn't until 1996 that we recruited bloodstock from our retired horses in training. Kabayil had won seven races for us and had a lovely pedigree. She was an ideal candidate. Her first foal was a colt named Dancing Bay and he won on the Flat at 3 years and 4 years whilst trained by Julie Camacho. He then embarked on a dual purpose career with Nicky Henderson and continued his winning ways.

Ffestiniog won several races for us including a Listed Race at Newbury and therefore acquired 'black type'. She became an ideal broodmare candidate for our programme and was immediately added when retired from racing. Having a Listed mare moved us a few more rungs up the ladder. Hopes were high that she would produce something special. In the event, her colt (Boston Lodge) didn't turn out to be star material, although we could hardly complain with three wins as a two-year-old.

Meanwhile, hiding in the shadows was another Club winner, Kalinka (Soviet Star). Her first offspring, Baralinka (Barathea) won on her debut. Perhaps a degree of complacency had crept in, nobody suspected or expected that she would be capable of producing the stuff that dreams are made of, just one year later. In February 2000, Kalinka produced a filly foal by Marju. She produced a Group 1 winner, Soviet Song.

Kalinka

In 2001 we added another two broodmares, Generous Diana (Generous) and Swiss Oaks winner Vent d'Aout (Imp Society).

As you would expect, visits to see the mares and foals are popular with Club members.

Kirtlington Stud is based near Oxford and, at the time of writing, is home to Ffestiniog, Generous Diana and Vent d'Aout.

Kabayil and Kalinka are in former trainer Maurice Camacho's care in North Yorkshire.

The foals stay at these locations until they are yearlings and move to their appointed trainers, towards the end of September.

The weekly newsletter keeps members up-to-date with all the news on the breeding front. Maurice Camacho's reports are a joy to behold and despite being a busy commercial enterprise, Kirtlington also provide interesting reports.

A Kirtlington Stud stable visit

Baralinka

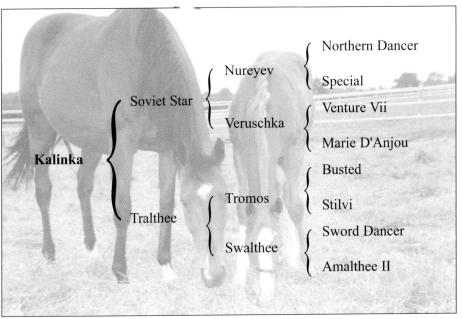

Kalinka

- Soviet Star
  - Nureyev
    - Northern Dancer
    - Special
  - Veruschka
    - Venture Vii
    - Marie D'Anjou
- Tralthee
  - Tromos
    - Busted
    - Stilvi
  - Swalthee
    - Sword Dancer
    - Amalthee II

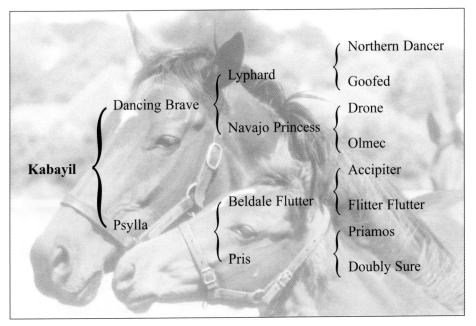

Kabayil

- Dancing Brave
  - Lyphard
    - Northern Dancer
    - Goofed
  - Navajo Princess
    - Drone
    - Olmec
- Psylla
  - Beldale Flutter
    - Accipiter
    - Flitter Flutter
  - Pris
    - Priamos
    - Doubly Sure

Most Stylish

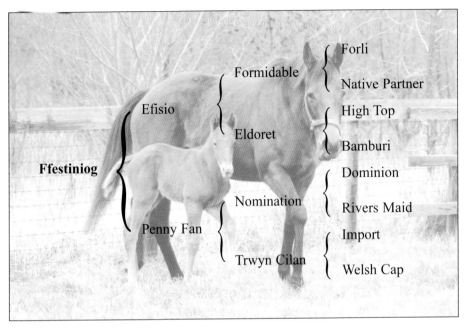

Ffestiniog

Efisio
- Formidable
  - Forli
  - Native Partner
- Eldoret
  - High Top
  - Bamburi

Penny Fan
- Nomination
  - Dominion
  - Rivers Maid
- Trwyn Cilan
  - Import
  - Welsh Cap

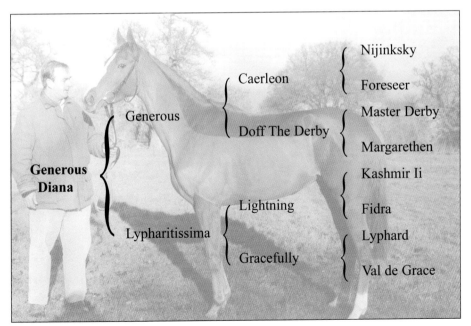

Generous Diana

Generous
- Caerleon
  - Nijinksky
  - Foreseer
- Doff The Derby
  - Master Derby
  - Margarethen

Lypharitissima
- Lightning
  - Kashmir Ii
  - Fidra
- Gracefully
  - Lyphard
  - Val de Grace

17

Kasamba

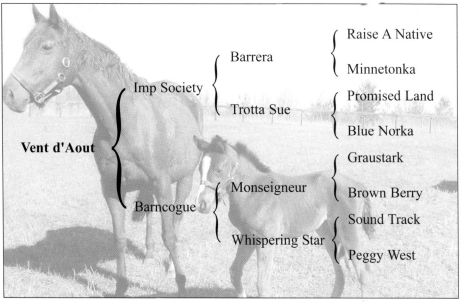

Vent d'Aout
- Imp Society
  - Barrera
    - Raise A Native
    - Minnetonka
  - Trotta Sue
    - Promised Land
    - Blue Norka
- Barncogue
  - Monseigneur
    - Graustark
    - Brown Berry
  - Whispering Star
    - Sound Track
    - Peggy West

EX-BROODMARES

Corman-Style
- Ahonoora
  - Lorenzaccio
  - Helen Nichols
- Miss Millicent
  - Milesian
  - Miss Pepita

Dixie Favor
- Dixieland Band
  - Northern Dancer
  - Mississippi Mud
- Femme Favor
  - Forli
  - Lady Parida

Vent D'Aout

Ffestiniog
Won her maiden at Folkestone in June 1997 over 6 furlongs. She won again next time out at Ascot, but her best performance came in October that year when she landed the Listed Radley Stakes at Newbury over seven furlongs. A number of placed efforts followed and she finished her career on a high, winning on her final ever start in October 1998.

Generous Diana
After three promising efforts, she lost her maiden tag over nine furlongs at Lingfield in October 1999. She went on to win a further two races over ten furlongs.

Kalinka
Won on her second ever start, landing a seven furlong Warwick maiden by three and a half lengths. Despite not getting her head in front again, she ran some good races in decent company and even tried her hand over hurdles for Charles Egerton.

Kabayil
A durable and tough performer, Kabayil won a novice hurdle at Plumpton over 2 miles 1 furlong in February 1993. She won another four times that year over two and two and a half miles. She won twice more for the Club over the next couple of years and also ran in two Cheltenham Festivals.

Vent d'Aout
Ran twice in France before scoring on her hurdling debut in Britain at Hereford in 1997 by twenty-three lengths and won a further three hurdle races. She ran a creditable sixth in the Elite Racing Club Triumph Hurdle at the Cheltenham Festival in 1998 and also won three times over fences.

Lord Oaksey

LORD OAKSEY

Elite Racing Club, President

Born, John Lawrence, 21st March 1929. Educated Eton, New College Oxford and Yale Law School. He chose to bypass the legal profession for his love of horseracing.

John's father, the Hon. Geoffrey Lawrence was presiding judge at the Nuremberg Trials of Nazi war criminals and was rewarded with a hereditary peerage as Lord Oaksey, the title which John inherited on his father's death.

In 1957 John became racing correspondent to The Daily Telegraph. At the same time his enthusiasm for amateur race riding was growing and his ability was there for all to see when becoming champion National Hunt amateur 1957-8 season. His highest profile wins were on Taxidermist (Hennessy and Whitbread Gold Cups).

His biggest disappointment was being beaten in the 1963 Grand National on Carrickbeg. He was the leader over the last fence and went clear on the run-in but just ran out of steam in the shadow of the winning post, beaten by the 66-1 outsider Ayala.

In 1964 John was a founder trustee of The Injured Jockeys Fund and became chairman in 1982.

As well as writing a weekly column for Horse & Hound magazine (as Audax), John was a regular member of the Channel Four Racing team for many years.

In 2001 John had the distinction of being elected an honorary member of The Jockey Club.

To have such a distinguished and knowledgeable Club President is an honour and enormous pleasure.

Ionian Spring

Some people may question why we use so many different trainers, when we employ our own trainer (Clive Cox) and have our own yard in Lambourn.

There are two main reasons for this policy. Firstly, Club members are spread throughout Great Britain thereby making it possible for many of them to make a stable visit without having to travel too far. Secondly, if a yard contracts a virus, the action can continue elsewhere.

When we look for a new trainer we are looking for a good communicator as well as a person with flair and aptitude. This person must not be frightened to tell us everything. Some trainers don't like to relay bad news about the horses.

We are only interested in 'warts and all' reports. We recognise that it takes a great deal of work and some good fortune just to get a racehorse to the racecourse, let alone into the winner's enclosure. Bad news generally outweighs the good. Maintaining a string of twenty horses in training helps counter the negatives. It is quite rare that all of the horses will be out of action at any particular time of the year.

The babies (two-year-olds) are particularly prone to illness. The National Hunt horses can have countless minor setbacks, often connected with the chaotic British weather.

Miracle Kid

JULIE CAMACHO

Julie comes from one of the North's most famous racing families and trains her small but select string near Malton in Yorkshire.

PAUL COLE

Our long association has resulted in plenty of quality action, notably his handling of Ffestiniog. 1991 Derby winner Generous was one of Paul's greatest horses.

CLIVE COX

Clive was assistant to the late Mikie Heaton-Ellis for seven years and took over when Mikie sadly died. He now trains from our own yard in Lambourn, which boasts superb facilities.

CHARLES EGERTON

Charles is a talented trainer and handled the late Mysilv for us with great success. Other jumping stars trained by Charles have included Shadow Leader, Decoupage and Teaatral.

Iambe De La See

JAMES **FANSHAWE**

James was a former assistant trainer to Sir Michael Stoute before taking out his licence in the early Nineties. James trains from the famous Pegasus Stables in Newmarket, built by Fred Archer. He has already trained the winner of two Champion Hurdles.

NICKY **HENDERSON**

Nicky has a quite remarkable record in the top races. He gained his first Cheltenham Festival win with See You Then in 1985 and now trains from his impressive Seven Barrows Stables near Lambourn.

ALAN **KING**

Alan was a former assistant to David Nicholson before taking over at Jackdaws and then moving to Barbury Castle. Alan has made a fantastic start and is sure to become a huge name.

LEN **LUNGO**

Len has made a successful transition from jockey to trainer since setting up his own purpose built yard overlooking the Solway Estuary in Scotland.

Alabang

One of the biggest winners the Club has ever experienced, was as the result of a three-way move amongst a group of trainers.

Our involvement in the training business began as a means of getting Club Members more involved in the racing world. It just seemed like a good idea to hire a trainer, lease a yard and fill it with racehorses. We were under no illusion that it would take some time before it could be turned into a profitable business.

It didn't take long before our intentions were widely known and we had many applications from trainers who were willing to take on the task. Eventually we chose Richard Phillips, who happened to be leasing a 32 box yard (Beechdown) and extensive gallops from John Francome. We had a deal with Richard and we became the new owners of the lease. This arrangement provided the perfect set-up. However, within a short time, Richard was offered a plum job to run the prestigious Gloucestershire training establishment, Jackdaws Castle.

Within hours of Richard's decision, Clive Cox became aware of the situation and suggested that he would be an ideal candidate to take over.

At the time, Clive was training at Barbury Castle, near Swindon. He had inherited the business from the late Mikie Heaton-Ellis, with whom he had acted as assistant trainer and indeed learnt his trade.

Meanwhile, Alan King was moving out of Jackdaws and was interested in taking over Barbury Castle. So Richard moved out of Beechdown and into Jackdaws, Clive moved to us and Alan moved in to Barbury Castle. The three-way move happened almost at the same time. A very neat arrangement and everyone was happy.

Knighted

At the time of writing, Alan still remains at Barbury Castle (and has now become an Elite Racing Club trainer). Richard moved out of Jackdaws to make way for Jonjo O'Neill and of course Clive Cox remains firmly entrenched at Beechdown.

When Clive, Tina and their two daughters moved to Beechdown, John Francome kindly agreed to knock the two semi-detached stable staff houses into one, thus providing a truly wonderful family home.

The main stable block is an American Barn, housing 30 horses. Clive's first week was spent gutting the place and with an army of helpers, they managed to paint the entire inside.

It didn't take long to find enough clients to fill the place and before we knew it, the place was thriving and making a small profit. Quite an achievement.

Small training establishments notoriously find it very difficult to make the business of training racehorses pay. Overheads, such as staff, computers and telephones, can make it almost an impossibility.

Clive does have a secret, it's all about a fabulous team effort plus respect for the staff and most importantly providing a superb environment for the horses. When you visit the yard, you cannot miss the fact that the horses are in great condition and if they could whisper in your ear, they would be asking you to put in a good word for an extended stay at Hotel Beechdown.

Being reasonably centrally located at Lambourn (the valley of the racehorse), Beechdown is a must for a visit. When you arrive, you will immediately sense how busy the whole place is. This is a full working racing yard. A stable visit starts with Members and their guests gathering in the huge indoor school. A selection of horses are worked by the stable staff including Clive. Then it's on to the gallops, where a stiff chilly wind generally seems to be the order of the day and expect it to be positively freezing a full three quarters of the year.

Global Search

This hardiness is an experience that most will endure in such awe that the long trek and inconvenience of inhospitable weather is accepted with a sort of gratitude. Can you just imagine getting up at 5am every day and working four lots in such conditions? These horsey people are certainly hardy individuals.

For Clive, as trainer, there's an added requirement. Every horse needs to be looked at twice a day. He will feel their legs, hoping and praying he will not find heat or any other ailment (the list of which is far too long to include here). These racehorses may be big robust looking individuals, but in reality they are a bunch of delicate actors, rehearsing their parts in a stage play that will be witnessed by thousands. Perfect athleticism is the requirement for each act of this play and it cannot be achieved if the horse has some imperfection.

The value of each hotel resident is far too great to take a single risk. Some horses do not even make it to the racecourse in an entire season.

Whilst the racehorses are unquestionably the stars of the show, take time to observe the staff. They beaver away, giving the impression that they are unaware of being watched by the visitors.

Stable lads and lasses are essential to the working of any yard and without them, there would simply not be any racing, anywhere.

Your visit to Beechdown will help you realise the considerable amount of work involved in preparing a horse for a racecourse appearance. If you are grateful for their efforts and admire their hard work, tell them! Such recognition is always appreciated.

It would help the staff if basic safety factors are observed when visiting the yard. Flash photography can seriously disturb a horse. Sudden movements, such as putting up an umbrella can disturb these highly-strung athletes.

Favorisio

Taking our own yard as an example. Individual owners pay us quite considerable sums to keep just one horse in training. Why do they do this? What is the attraction when the statistics are stacked so heavily against making a profit from the venture?

Firstly, you must of course be able to afford to write-off the expenditure with a greater gusto than buying a brand new car. You certainly don't enter the world of racehorse ownership in the hope of turning this sporting extravaganza into a cast iron investment. In fact approximately 94% of all racehorses fail to win enough prize money to pay their annual training and racing expenses. Of the remaining 6%, less than 0.1% will become worth a small fortune and those that do achieve star status, are rarely found by chance in the sale ring for a sum less than £50,000.

Armed with all this knowledge, one must conclude that the overwhelming attraction is the challenge of getting into the winner's enclosure, anywhere. A thrill that never loses its appeal.

Unfortunately, for some owners, a sentimental bonding is formed with the racehorse. Could it be that the happiness these horses exude in their expensive suites and the effervescent mollycoddling from the hotel staff, results in a belief that the owner owes the horse a duty never to let him or her be subjected to an inferior environment. The owner does not hear the trainer utter the words, "this horse is not good enough, he should be retired". The owner cannot bear to think of his Nijinski relegated to a paddock position alongside Nancy Smith's 23year old pony, ten chickens and a goat.

The reality is that some horses do not enjoy being racehorses. A good trainer will identify such individuals and advise the owner accordingly. Elite Racing Club has had its fair share of unenthusiastic performers. The most notorious of which being an expensive female purchase ingratiated with the very racehorsey name of Pharazini. This little madam was a star on paper and even looked the proverbial million dollars, but was clearly trying to lay claim to a leading part in a Hamlet cigar commercial.

Shining Oasis

She would slide into the stalls without hitch or hindrance but would then seek the attention of all, by dramatically refusing to budge from her open stall. On the rare occasions that she did decide to give punters a run for their money she proved an ability worthy of her glamorous looks. Eventually, enough was enough and her paddock place was booked.

In a nutshell, the pure racehorse owner (he who owns a whole horse) should be prepared for all eventualities and most definitely not enter this game if finances would be dented with any noticeable force.

The Elite Racing Club slogan (the next best thing to your own racehorse), could arguably be quite wrong. Members do not have any financial involvement or responsibility for the string of horses. There cannot be any unexpected vet bill etc..... Could it be BETTER than your own racehorse? Every individual member is one of the connections. You are sharing those famous black and white colours. The fact that there are thousands of others enjoying the entertainment, diminishes the experience not one jot.

For the doubting few, let them witness a visit to the Club's yard, every Club member is treated just like any individual owner. And this is just a part of the whole experience of membership.

Statistically, the Club was in the top 45 of all racehorse owners through-out 2002, on the basis of quantity of horses in training. Not bad, given that the total number of registered owners was in the region of 9,250, with over half only owning one horse.

Lady For Life

Given that there can never be a guarantee that any of the Club's horses will ever win another race, it follows that not one ounce of reliance should ever be placed on receiving a single penny dividend at the end of your year's membership.

In reality of course, there is an expectation of winning prize money and without exception every penny of prize money paid by Weatherbys (administrators of racing on behalf of The Jockey Club) to Elite Racing Club is divided equally amongst the members.

Weatherbys statements appear every week in the newsletter. These accounts are a real eye-opener. The costs of racing one horse is huge. Multiply this by 20 and the figures become staggering.

For years, an argument has reigned in respect of prize money. Many members have argued that it is pointless dividing it up. Putting the funds back into bloodstock would seem more appropriate, they claim. In fact, we insist that the prize money goes back to the members. In 2002 members who renewed were offered a 15% loyalty discount, plus, effectively a further almost 15% dividend, further offsetting the next 12 months fee. This is surely enough to prove the worth of dividing the prize money won.

Given the Jockey Club statistic of 94% of racehorses failing to make a profit annually, we believe that the return in 2002 was a remarkably excellent achievement, and there have been other excellent years. But do remember that there can never be any guarantee of any specific percentage dividend in the future. Having said that, we will of course always be attempting to surpass our best.

Elite Racing

You can't get any better inside information on the well-being and fitness of a racehorse, than from the trainer.

The truth is that the majority of all racehorses are fit and raring to go, when they are declared to run in a race. In fact, no horse should be taking part in any race unless it is fit enough to do so.

The Club employs betting experts to complement the inside information from the trainer. It's all very well and, of course, most helpful to hear our trainer enthusing over the winning chance of a horse, but that doesn't create a certainty. Every other horse in the race could be at peak fitness and be lined up by equally enthusiastic trainers. The form of the other horses in the race needs to be researched and a further analysis of how our horse will act on the prevailing ground conditions is absolutely vital.

After carrying out their assessment of the horse's chance in the race, our betting experts will formulate a percentage chance of winning. This percentage is then converted to betting odds, which can then be interpreted as value for money. For example; if the percentage chance of winning was 50%, that equates to even money. If the bookmakers then offered 4-7 that would hardly represent good value. You don't need to consult a conversion chart to determine that one. However, it really does help if you become familiar with the conversion figures. This is second nature for every bookmaker in the land, yet for some reason, punters rarely care. Hardly surprising, therefore, that so many punters bet at odds that represent appalling value for money. The long term effect of which is that the bookmaker makes a healthy profit at the punter's expense. Going back to the example of the 4-7 odds, the conversion figure is 63.64%, a difference of 13.64% with evens (50%). When you start looking at longer odds, 12-1 and 20-1, for example, they may seem miles away from each other but they are actually only 2.93% apart. In other words, the shorter the odds the more one should watch the value element.

Lord High Admiral

The word 'bookmaker' means; 'a person who forms a book on the outcome of an event'. This 'book' is an accounting method of calculating percentage chances of all the possible outcomes in an event, to achieve a minimum of 100%. If the bookmaker fails to construct a book of at least 100% it means that punters can place bets on every outcome to guarantee a profit. Therefore the cardinal rule of the bookmaking profession is to always achieve a minimum of 100% and normally a figure of around 115%. Whatever, the percentage figure is, greater than 100%, becomes the 'overround'. This, in theory, guarantees the bookmaker a profit at the punter's expense. In other words the odds are always stacked against the punter.

Elite Racing Club members are not discouraged from betting. It's a fact that betting enhances the enjoyment of horseracing. Never bet more than you can afford to lose and always treat your betting as an entertainment.

Some new members have joined the Club at a time that coincides with a run of winners. The betting experts may also have been spot-on with their advice. This can be rather dangerous, as the impression could be that the Club is the answer to that elusive quest to break the bookie's bank. Just remember that horses are not machines and there's no such thing as a certainty.

Your task should be to try to beat the bookie at his own game. You manipulate the odds in your favour and when the value is simply not there, you don't bet.

Elite Hope

Odds On	Price	Odds Against	Odds On	Price	Odds Against
50.00	Evens	50.00	87.50	7/1	12.50
52.38	11/10	47.62	88.24	15/2	11.76
54.55	6/5	45.45	88.89	8/1	11.11
55.56	5/4	44.44	89.47	17/2	10.53
57.89	11/8	42.11	90.00	9/1	10.00
60.00	6/4	40.00	90.91	10/1	9.09
61.90	13/8	38.10	91.67	11/1	8.33
63.64	7/4	36.36	92.31	12/1	7.69
65.22	15/8	34.78	92.86	13/1	7.14
66.67	2/1	33.33	93.33	14/1	6.67
68.00	85/40	32.00	93.75	15/1	6.25
69.23	9/4	30.77	94.12	16/1	5.88
71.43	5/2	28.57	95.24	20/1	4.76
73.33	11/4	26.67	95.65	22/1	4.35
75.00	3/1	25.00	96.15	25/1	3.85
76.92	100/30	23.08	97.06	33/1	2.94
77.78	7/2	22.22	97.56	40/1	2.44
80.00	4/1	20.00	98.04	50/1	1.96
81.81	9/2	18.18	98.51	66/1	1.49
83.33	5/1	16.67	98.77	80/1	1.23
84.62	11/2	15.38	99.01	100/1	0.99
85.71	6/1	14.29	99.60	250/1	0.40
86.67	13/2	13.33	99.80	500/1	0.20

Latin Leader

Crowd scene at Ascot 1904

This was the scene at Ascot racecourse circa 1904. In those times crowds were huge, yet transport was not as convenient as today, but of course, if you wanted to see live racing, the only option was to be there.

Nowadays, the BHB (British Horseracing Board) are throwing millions of pounds at the task of getting the crowds back to the racecourses. Satellite racing channels, internet and technological devices counter the BHB activity.

We would like to think that Elite Racing Club is playing its part in helping to encourage more people to go racing.

We have secured great deals with some racecourses. On 1,000 Guineas day at Newmarket 2003, they had their biggest crowd since records began. Over 1,000 tickets were sold by us at a 35% discount to members.

Other good discounts have been secured at important meetings such as the Cheltenham Festival, for example.

Pomme Secret

Elite Racing Club representative Kay Bliss, with Charles Egerton and members at Bath

Going to the races and joining the trainer and jockey in the paddock is an experience to be savoured. Every member is given the opportunity to enjoy this benefit, on a rota basis.

A simple automated telephone system (non-premium rate) is linked to a computer in the office and this allocates places on the day of the race.

Some enthusiastic members visit the paddock on a regular basis.

Demand is obviously greater for Ascot than some smaller venues, however, with so many runners at so many racecourses, it is not difficult to find a suitable opportunity.

We also do our best to organise trips (at cost) when we have a runner abroad.

A dress code applies to all members at every racecourse when accepting a paddock/winners enclosure place. Gentlemen are expected to wear collar and tie and ladies are expected to be smart. This policy has been universally accepted and is here to stay.

Cherished

For those who enjoy getting out and about, there are plenty of hospitality events, organised in conjunction with stable visits and various race meetings.

We have a team of people who organise and attend these events. They have become experts in buying the events at a reasonable cost and designing packages that represent exceptionally good value for money.

For example; for over five years we have been organising a package (three course meal, private marquee, bar, tote and guest speaker) on Gold Cup day at The Cheltenham Festival, at considerably less than commercially structured packages.

Any racecourse that is prepared to offer a sensibly priced deal, is considered by our hospitality team. This means that there's a wide choice of venues.

Hospitality events are not linked to every stable visit but are becoming more popular. The procedure is that the visit will normally be any time between 9am and 11am and then a local hotel or restaurant will be booked for lunch. Once again, the team do their best to obtain a value for money deal.

Elite Racing Club Hospitality with Lord Oaksey

Stately Favour

One of the biggest expenses the Club endures is the production, printing and despatch of the weekly newsletter. It's a mammoth task to produce such a quality product, week after week, but a task that the Club thrives on.

Every week the trainers inform us of the well being of each horse. Knowing how each one is performing at home is absolutely vital information. This weekly information builds a comprehensive picture and those who like to have a bet can prepare themselves.

The newsletter keeps a close watch on all the horses in the breeding programme. The progress of mares, yearlings and foals is both fascinating and educational.

Possible future races for the Club horses is an important feature, as well as all the in depth results.

Perhaps one of the most interesting features is 'Members Correspondence'. This provides an opportunity for Members to make suggestions for improvements and to sound-off about this, that and the other. It would be fair to say that the Club has its fair share of expert 'armchair jockeys' who seem to know-all and are only too willing to inform our jockeys where they went wrong if we don't manage a win.

The newsletter is an entirely in-house production. Time is a vital factor. We cannot afford to risk printing or production delays so we have our own print factory at a local trading estate. A typical production schedule would be for the writing team to compile throughout the week, then the editor will put the finishing touches to the text by Monday morning. Then by Monday evening, our studio will have set the text ready for printing. By Tuesday 11am, the printing will be completed and passed to the finishing department, who take several hours to collate, bind and stitch the finished product. The final task is to pack and post the newsletter, which is often concluded by Tuesday night.

British Racecourses

Aintree (NH)	Market Rasen (NH)
Ascot (F, NH)	Musselburgh (F, NH)
Ayr (F, NH)	Newbury (F, NH)
Bangor (NH)	Newcastle (F, NH)
Bath (F)	Newmarket (F)
Beverley (F)	Newton Abbot (NH)
Brighton (F)	Nottingham (F)
Carlisle (F, NH)	Perth (NH)
Cartmel (NH)	Plumpton (NH)
Catterick (F, NH)	Pontefract (F)
Cheltenham (NH)	Redcar (F)
Chepstow (F, NH)	Ripon (F)
Chester (F)	Salisbury (F)
Doncaster (F, NH)	Sandown (F, NH)
Epsom (F)	Sedgefield (NH)
Exeter (NH)	Southwell (F, NH, AW)
Fakenham (NH)	Stratford (NH)
Folkestone (F, NH)	Taunton (NH)
Fontwell (NH)	Thirsk (F)
Goodwood (F)	Towcester (NH)
Hamilton (F)	Uttoxeter (NH)
Haydock (F, NH)	Warwick (F, NH)
Hereford (NH)	Wetherby (NH)
Hexham (NH)	Wincanton (NH)
Huntingdon (NH)	Windsor (F)
Kelso (NH)	Wolverhampton (F, AW)
Kempton (F, NH)	Worcester (NH)
Leicester (F, NH)	Yarmouth (F)
Lingfield (F, NH, AW)	York (F)
Ludlow (NH)	

F = Flat   NH = National Hunt   AW = All-Weather

Seixo Branco

We are offered photographs of Club horses from many professional sources and normally agree terms to purchase the copyright of the images. There can be many occasions when we purchase photographs and never use them.

Given that we handle so many photographs, this has become a major expense and we attempt to recoup some of this cost by offering some prints for sale.

Most newsletter covers have a full colour photograph. We are rarely pushed to find a suitable subject.

One of our favourite photographs, Pomme Secret in the 1997 Triumph Hurdle.

Elite Justice

From time to time we commission a painting of a Club horse. This is a far more costly exercise than a photograph but can result in a collectible treasure for Club Members.

Prints of the painting are advertised in the newsletter, whenever available, and are sold at realistic prices.

The work below is by Richard Bliss. Titled; Fighting Spirit.

Persian Elite

Following the career of an apprentice can be quite fascinating. Since the earliest days of Elite Racing Club, we have endeavoured to sponsor an up-and-coming young rider. In exchange for financial help, the apprentice undertakes to supply regular reports for the newsletter.

Alan, Aimee and Pat Eddery

Alan Daly and Aimee Cook are pictured here with Pat Eddery at Windsor on the day we launched the apprentice sponsorship scheme.

Alan went on to become a well known jockey. Aimee Cook has yet to make a name for herself as a jockey but will never forget her first ever winner on the Club's Persian Elite (see opposite). It was a day that will never be forgotten by her family. The emotions were overwhelming and there was no prouder father than former top jockey Paul Cook.

Other former sponsored apprentices have been Glen Sparkes and Robert Winston. At the time of writing, Liverpool lad, Ashley Hindley, (attached to trainer Clive Cox) is the man of the moment.

Ffestiniog

The list of jockeys who have ridden for Elite Racing Club is seemingly endless.

And as well as the star names, there have been some not so well-known names, such as Polly Gundry who notched up four wins with Empire Park.

Here are just a few of the jockeys who have ridden for the Club:-

DEAN **CORBY**

Arguably one of the most talented apprentice jockeys of recent times and winner of the 2002 Championship, Corby is indentured to Mick Channon's stable. He rode Boston Lodge to win a competitive and valuable Nursery at Epsom in August 2002.

FRANKIE **DETTORI**

Frankie rode our 75th winner when partnering Paradise Navy to victory at Yarmouth in October 1997. He is probably best known for riding every winner on a seven race card at Ascot in September 1996, not to mention his flying dismounts. He has steered home a whole host of top horses over the last ten years, including Barathea (1994 Breeders' Cup Mile), Mark Of Esteem (1996 Queen Elizabeth II Stakes), Singspiel (1996 Japan Cup), Fantastic Light (2001 Breeders' Cup Turf) and Sakhee (2001 Prix de L'Arc de Triomphe).

Dont Tell The Wife

PAT **EDDERY**

Got off the mark for us when steering home Ionian Spring in a nine furlong handicap at Nottingham in March 2002. Eddery first came to prominence in 1975, when Grundy powered home in the English and Irish Derbys as well as the King George. Other wins include the 1982 Derby with Golden Fleece, the 1985 Champion Stakes with Pebbles, the 1986 King George with Dancing Brave and the 1996 1,000 Guineas with Bosra Sham. He has been Champion Jockey in Britain eleven times and he notched up 209 wins in 1990.

MICK **FITZGERALD**

As stable jockey for Nicky Henderson, Mick has ridden for the Club on a number of occasions. He has won five times whilst donning the famous black and white silks with Fanfaron, Iambe De La See (twice), Miracle Kid and Dancing Bay. Mick has won both the Grand National (Rough Quest) and Cheltenham Gold Cup (See More Business) and was leading jockey at the Cheltenham Festival in both 1999 and 2000.

BRIAN **HARDING**

Won a novice hurdle aboard Global Search in May 2000 by six lengths. Harding has had a highly successful career in the saddle and the highlight so far was probably when he partnered the housewives' favourite, One Man, to victory in the Queen Mother Champion Chase at Cheltenham in '98.

DAVID **HARRISON**

One of the most successful flat jockeys of the late 1990s. David Harrison has ridden a number of winners for Elite trainer James Fanshawe, notably Arctic Owl, triumphant in the 2000 Irish St Leger. He also partnered Travelmate to finish fifth in the 1999 Melbourne Cup. Harrison rode many winners in Hong Kong and landed the 1999 Derby aboard Holy Grail. Seriously injured in a fall at Sha Tin in 2001, at the time of writing, Harrison is still receiving intensive physiotherapy.

Cross Talk

RICHARD **HUGHES**

Has ridden three winners for the Club, including our 50th, at Bath in 1996 aboard Paradise Navy. Hughes is the son of Cheltenham winning jump jockey and trainer Dessie. He rides regularly for Mick Channon and his father-in-law Richard Hannon and is retained by high-profile owner, Khalid Abdulla. His first Group 1 success came in the 1995 Gran Premio d'Italia aboard Paul Cole's Posidonas.

JOHN **KAVANAGH**

In November 2001, he steered Miracle Kid home for a well-deserved victory in a handicap hurdle at Warwick. Kavanagh rides predominantly for Elite trainer Nicky Henderson.

JIMMY **MCCARTHY**

Has ridden four winners for the Club, with Dont Tell The Wife being the first back in 1996. He has won on both Fanfaron and Seixo Branco for Charles Egerton and also rode Lady For Life to victory at Hereford in 1999, notching up the Club's 100th winner.

TONY **MCCOY**

The most successful jump jockey of all time has won six times for the Club, including twice with Vent d'Aout, who is now a broodmare. He has also ridden winners on Pomme Secret and Lady For Life. McCoy has won all three big races at the Cheltenham Festival, the Champion Hurdle (Make A Stand) and Gold Cup (Mr Mulligan) in 1997 and the Queen Mother Champion Chase in 2000 with Edredon Bleu. He broke Sir Gordon Richards's fifty year-old record for most wins in a season in 2002, when he partnered Valfonic to victory in a novice hurdle at Warwick.

Hamilton Silk

MICHAEL **ROBERTS**

Roberts began his career in South Africa, where he was champion jockey eleven times. He first came over to Britain in 1976 and his big race wins include the 1991 2,000 Guineas on Mystiko and the 1993 Oaks with Intrepidity. Other big race wins include the 1993 Irish 2,000 Guineas aboard champion miler Barathea. He has an excellent record for Elite Racing Club and he has won five times for us, including three times on Lord High Admiral. He retired in May 2002 due to medical reasons.

OSCAR **URBINA**

2002 turned out to be a memorable year for the Spanish jockey. After giving Soviet Song the perfect racing introduction at Kempton in July, he then rode her to a brilliant success in the Listed Sweet Solera Stakes at Newmarket. They went on to win the Group 1 Meon Valley Stud Fillies' Mile at Ascot in September the same year, giving the Club and Oscar their first Group 1 winner. Urbina first started working for James Fanshawe in 1999 after a five year spell with fellow Newmarket trainer, Luca Cumani.

JASON **WEAVER**

Had a relatively short but distinguished career, winning eight Group 1 races in total. Retired in 2001, he is probably best known for his successes aboard both Double Trigger and Mister Baileys, the latter winning the 1994 2,000 Guineas.

NORMAN **WILLIAMSON**

The Irishman has ridden for the Club on many occasions and has recorded wins on Empire Park, Seixo Branco, Alabang and Mysilv. He achieved the notable Champion Hurdle and Gold Cup double in 1995 with Alderbrook and Master Oats respectively. He was also a close second in the 2000 Grand National, when Mely Moss lost out by a length and a quarter. He decided to move back to his homeland in 2002 but he continues to ride winners on both sides of the Irish Sea.

Mysilv

By 1994 the Club had not managed to acquire a star racehorse. Then an opportunity came our way when Triumph Hurdle winner Mysilv was reluctantly offered by a syndicate of owners, who had originally agreed to sell the horse after a given period of time.

She was offered at The Doncaster Sales and we were represented by trainer Charles Egerton. As the bidding climbed over the £125,000 mark, it was just us and the mighty Coolmore Stud left to fight it out. We were determined to acquire this fabulous mare and indeed we did, setting a world record for a National Hunt horse in training (the final bill amounting to £162,750).

The next day, our purchase was front page news in The Racing Post and just about every national newspaper reported our acquisition. Yet it was a full seven months before she was ready to race in the black and white silks.

Mysilv in The 1996 Stayers' Hurdle

Her first outing was not expected to be a winning one and indeed she trailed in last of six at Kempton, in the Grade 1 Christmas Hurdle in 1994. Our game chestnut mare soon bounced back however and she went on to win her next two starts, including the 1995 Tote Gold Trophy at Newbury. She went on to finish fifth in that year's Champion Hurdle.

Sadly, the 1995/1996 season turned out to be her last. Mysilv seemed to be at the top of her game however and she finished either first or second in every race that season, apart from the Champion Hurdle, where she was sixth behind Collier Bay.

Two days after her exertions in the Champion Hurdle, trainer Charles Egerton decided to run her in the Stayers' Hurdle and after a brave fight, she went down by just three-quarters of a length to Cyborgo. This was an amazing performance and in what turned out to be her last ever race, she finished second again, this time in the French Champion Hurdle at Auteuil.

During a routine work out on the gallops over Christmas 1996, Mysilv inexplicably fractured her pelvis and had to be put down. Naturally, everyone at Elite Racing Club and the many thousands of members were absolutely devastated, it came as a huge shock to everyone involved. Mysilv was Elite Racing Club's first star horse and her legacy was one of fantastic memories and a hope that one day we would find another horse equally as brave and talented.

Soviet Song

This filly began life in North Yorkshire, the second foal of the Club's broodmare Kalinka. Little did we realise that we had a Group 1 winner on our hands.

She was the last of the homebreds to be found a home in October 2001. We decided to add James Fanshawe to our list of trainers and she was sent to him.

By March 2002, James was cautiously optimistic that she would make a nice racehorse. In July, she had her first outing and was up against a well-touted newcomer called Airwave. Soviet Song could do no better than win and one could argue that jockey Oscar Urbina had a little more up his sleeve.

This was a win in decent company. James was beginning to think a lot of her but still remained cautiously optimistic. A good test would be a stab at a Listed race and he went for The Sweet Solera at Newmarket on 10 August. She won the race well and cautious optimism turned into quite high hopes.

Her next target was The Meon Valley Stud Fillies Mile, a Group 1 race at Ascot. This would determine whether or not she was star material. A brilliant ride from Oscar Urbina resulted in a cosy win and she fulfilled the Club's long term dream of achieving a Group 1 win. The fact that she was also homebred was the icing on the cake.

As winter (2002) approached, many of the leading bookmakers were quoting her joint favourite for the 1,000 Guineas. She eventually started clear second favourite and finished a creditable 4th in a particularly well contested race.

Rebel County

Once a Club racehorse has been retired from racing, we endeavour to find a loving new home.

Fortunately, we experience little difficulty giving such horses away, including to Club members, on the understanding that each horse will not be raced again.

To qualify for consideration, the member must have a sound knowledge of the thoroughbred and be a competent rider. He or she must also have suitable accommodation for the horse.

Once the horse has been given away, we ask that the new owner supplies the occasional report (for the newsletter). This enables members to keep track of how our old friends are progressing.

The picture below is of the successfully re-homed Club favourite Paradise Navy. As well as having the distinction of running in The Derby, he was also the winner of many races.

Stirrup Cup

Captain Bliss

New Seeker

Ionian Spring

Bayrak

Favorisio

Boston Lodge

Pomme Secret

Bid For Fame

Pacific Grove

Reims

Spencers Revenge

Dancing Bay

Soviet Song

Colonial Sunrise

Vocation

Lord High Admiral

Dungarvans Choice

Ffestiniog

Soviet Song

Kasamba

Alabang

Global Search

Baralinka

Kalinka

Vent D'Aout

Dungarvans Choice

Alzanti

Hamilton Silk

Baralinka

Young Snugfit

Paradise Navy

Pacific Grove

Knighted

Hamilton Silk

Empire Park

Fanfaron

Elite Hope

Colonial Sunrise

Soviet Song

Lord High Admiral

Royal Crest

Faugeron

Empire Park

Vent D'Aout

Young Snugfit

Fanfaron

Empire Park

Favorisio

THE EVENTING CLUB

Darrell Scaife and Captain Mumble en route to victory at Bicton, 2003

Darrell Scaife and Alfred Of Church Farm at Badminton

The Eventing Club was set up in March 2002 with one horse, Captain Mumble who is ridden and trained by international event rider Darrell Scaife. The major aim of The Eventing Club was to take all the applicable successful aspects of the Elite Racing Club and transfer them to another challenging equine discipline. Similar to the early ambitions of the Elite Racing Club, the hope is that one day we may have a horse talented enough to compete at Badminton and represent Britain in a major championship.

At the time of writing, members of Elite Racing Club are entitled to membership of The Eventing Club and can consequently enjoy the perks of event-horse ownership. As well as stable visits and the opportunity to watch the Club horse compete in beautiful surroundings all over Britain, members are kept fully up-to-date with the latest Club news via a non-premium rate hotline and website.

Captain Mumble's first event at Burnham Beeches in April 2002 was a highly promising debut and he finished a respectable twelfth. As the season progressed, Captain Mumble's experience and confidence grew and he won his first event at West Wilts Horse Trials in June. It was a wonderful moment for the members who attended and Captain Mumble relished the subsequent photo call! Further placings followed at both Brockenhurst Park and Mount Ballan.

Over the winter, Captain Mumble enjoyed a short holiday and then some intensive training sessions with Captain Mark Philips and Yogi Breisner. Darrell felt that the six year-old son of Australian Thoroughbred Woodmount Magic had really strengthened up over the winter and he was hoping for a successful campaign in 2003. The season got off to a solid start at Stilemans and then just one week later, Captain Mumble justified his supporters faith when he won at Bicton in very convincing fashion.

The Club has organised a number of interesting and entertaining days, including demonstrations by British Eventing's Performance Manager and jumping guru Yogi Breisner. Members have also been able to take advantage of cross-country course walks with Yogi and Darrell at Badminton and Gatcombe.

Darrell Scaife and Alfred of Church Farm at Blenheim

After Britain's dismal performance in the 1948 Olympics, the tenth Duke of Beaufort decided that he would host a three-day-event on his Badminton estate in Gloucestershire, in the hope that the home team would be better prepared for the 1952 Olympics in Helsinki. And so in April 1949 the sport of Eventing was launched in Britain, with just twenty-two competitors and a handful of spectators. As the event grew and interest increased, other competitions were slowly introduced and in 1951 Britain's first one-day-event was held.

The format of the three-day-event has remained largely unchanged for over sixty years and comprises of dressage (day one) cross-country (day two) and show jumping (day three). Dressage is performed in an arena (60 x 20 metres) and tests the suppleness and obedience of the horse and the skill and poise of the rider. As horse and rider progress through the grades (novice, intermediate, advanced), they are asked to complete more difficult movements in walk, trot and canter. In a three-day-event, each dressage movement (normally about 20) is given a mark out of ten by three separate judges. The marks obtained are converted to penalties by subtracting them from the maximum obtainable. So that dressage exerts the right amount of influence on the competition, the total penalties are converted to a percentage, to which a standard coefficient is applied. Therefore, the lower the score the better.

Horses and riders then progress to day two and carry their penalty scores forward to the cross-country. This is the ultimate test of horsemanship and is considered the most influential element of the competition and the most exciting for spectators. Horse and rider have to complete a cross-country course across a variety of terrain over natural and man-made obstacles. The length of the course varies depending on the level of competition. The horses have to complete the course in a set time and incur 0.4 time penalties for every second over the optimum time. Prior to the start of the cross-country, competitors have to complete two sections of roads and tracks and a steeplechase course. This acts as a warm up and as with the cross-country, penalties are incurred for exceeding the optimum times on each phase.

On the third day of the competition, horses are trotted up in front of the ground jury (dressage judges) and any horse not deemed sound is eliminated from the competition. Horse and rider then have to complete a course of show jumps and once again, this is timed and four penalties are added for each fence that is knocked down.

HOW TO JOIN
ELITE RACING CLUB

visit the website:

www.eliteracingclub.co.uk

<u>or</u> telephone
01380 811699

12 months membership costs £169
or 4 quarterly payments of £44.75